SELECTED
POEMS
FOR *Freedom*, *Peace*,
AND *Love*

SELECTED POEMS

FOR *Freedom*, *Peace*,

AND *Love*

LEONARD A. SLADE, JR.

XULON PRESS

Xulon Press
2301 Lucien Way #415
Maitland, FL 32751
407.339.4217
www.xulonpress.com

© 2020 by Leonard A. Slade, Jr.

Unless otherwise indicated, Scripture quotations taken from the King James Version (KJV) –*public domain.*

Printed in the United States of America.

ISBN-13: 978-1-6628-0269-0
Ebook: 978-1-6628-0270-6

For Roberta and Minitria

Table of Contents

Begin Writing the Poem

to produce sweat
and to boil blood.
No matter who reads
or doesn't, I'm a poet.
I'll always have something to say.
I write the truth
about the good
and the bad. Nothing
can stop my sword.
I'll continue with the poem
until maggots eat my eyeballs.
I'll return to the poem
that eats the flesh
or that kisses the soul.
And remember, there's war
in my heart, there's love, too
but don't find yourself
in the pit of the poem.
Love me and help me
fly.

Poetry

It creates beauty and truth,
exposes darkness destruction.
Sometimes it laughs
like a hyena.
In winter it buries the dead
with tears soaking souls
snow blankets earth
until spring arrives
flowers bloom
birds sing.
Once it hits the page
with feelings and
words,
Who knows where it will end?

For My Forefathers

For my forefathers
Whipped from Africa
Where children cried
But ships sailed on
And plantation owners were animals
Their roars echoing three-hundred years.

For my forefathers
Whose fingers pierced cotton bolls
Beneath the sun roasting human flesh
And darkness told master
To rape black women
for labor and profit.

For my forefathers
Whose masters cursed the North
And justified the South
And debated Lincoln vs. Douglass
And cited slaves in the Bible
And returned to Africa for more.

For my forefathers
Who couldn't read or write
But heard freedom ringing
After Lincoln's Emancipation Proclamation
That taught me to watch
And pray for a new day.

For my forefathers
who loved me.

Abraham Lincoln

He sucked a thumb in Kentucky,
where his father chopped wood
for warm evenings
in December. He wore old
clothes and walked barefoot
among lilacs in spring. And everywhere
he moved, Indiana and Illinois,
laughter filled the air

as young boys teased his height
and demeaned his clothes. No
child ever praised him,
and he for his suffering honored
her, all children thought small
of his future, except her
who read her Bible and loved him
as no other person could.

He studied by candlelight,
savoring words and defining dreams
for America. He was hungry for truth
and debated the pros and cons
of slavery. He promised a united country
but blood would taint freedom.
Brother against brother
sister against sister

blacks against whites
Northerners against Southerners –
they all fought for their cause.
Our father of freedom

bathed America with hope
and then was bathed himself
in cold blood.
Children cried.

I Came, I Saw, I Dreamed

(for Abraham Lincoln)

I see a child being born to save a country.
I see a spiritual giant being patient
      with a Southern belle.
I see a father grieving over the death of his child.
I hear cries and see tears showering the soul
      of a Nation.
I see parents sending their sons
      to fight for freedom.
I hear slaves praying and singing in the cotton fields.
I observe a U.S. President loved and hated,
      decisive and brave.
I see a country's savior, healing a people.
      divided by war, slain by an assassin's bullet.
I see a country strong and powerful, beautiful and blessed.
I dream a better world.

Thank You, Abe!

Abraham Lincoln set me free,
Gave me dignity for the world to see.
Some have said he did not care
About my blackness and the slavery affair.
But I sincerely and honestly believe
This man was called to help us breathe
Truth, righteousness, justice, and all.
America now stands proud and tall.
Thank you, Abe, for what you have done
For giving us victory that's almost won.

Elizabeth Keckley

I see Elizabeth Keckley working
As a seamstress for Abraham Lincoln,
Mary Todd being comforted by her,
A former slave suffering floggings,
Now sewing warm red clothes
For the restless First Lady.
Her mahogany body gracing
The White House, her voice sweet
With love in her heart,
She teaches The President
The beauty of Blackness,
The power of brotherhood.
I see a warrior,
I see a modiste,
I see a Saint
Singing in Heaven.

Phillis Wheatley

Classical in her treatment of poetry,
She published poems
To protest racism and
The bad behavior of students.
Brilliant with her structure of poems
And thematic development.
Here was a scholar
Who showed the world
What a black person
Could do with the pen
In the 1700's and 1800's
When slaves were prevented
From reading and writing.
Here was a writer,
Here was a genius,
Here was a giant,
For the ages.

Frederick Douglass

Like Frederick Douglass, I battle you,
stir your conscience, America,
so rich, with welfare and homelessness,
and crime galore, so much slavery now.

Like Douglass, I share biting truth, but
you open my heart, hoping for change, although
I smile at you through wrinkles of blood – you,
my sweet home, stir me to tears.

John Brown

The revolutionary's faith in freedom
      The power he shares;
The guns he carries for protection,
      He for some betrays.

His willingness kissing death,
      His words written in blood,
And actions speak for him,
      His heart knows truth.

But still he knows the future
      That freedom will come
For all who will make sacrifices
      The land must first soak in blood.

Harriet Tubman

"The Moses of Her People"
Led hundreds out of bondage.
She was called stupid
During a brutal childhood.
She worked in the fields
And escaped slavery
To become "the conductor"
Of the Underground Railroad.
Several Northern abolitionists
Supported her cause.
She was a cook
And a nurse and a spy.
"The Moses of Her People"
Died loving freedom.

Sojourner Truth

She spoke with thunder
Let my people go.
She fought for women's rights,
Bore thirteen children
Who were sold into slavery.
Her mystical vision was to travel
America to speak the truth
About slavery and freedom.
She sang gospel songs
And interrupted meetings
Protesting slavery and women's subjugation.
She said no to male chauvinism
And yes to freedom for all.
She died whispering
"I'm free, thank God!
I'm free, thank God!"

George Moses Horton

From Northampton County, North Carolina, a
slave labors on a farm;
he walks to the State University at Chapel Hill
writing love poems for students on weekends
to send home to their sweethearts,
money exchanged for the purchase of freedom.

Published poetry in newspapers,
books reflecting his genius
he studies Methodist hymns
how happy could readers be

when the Civil War ends
he travels to Philadelphia for respect
from the black bourgeoisie
books published for eternity
the whereabouts of his death
unknown.

I Am a Black Man

I am a Black man
my history written with blood
some sweet songs of sorrow
are composed for my soul
and I
can be seen plowing in the fields
Can be heard
humming
in the night

I saw my grandfather coming to America
and I reached back in time
to help him settle in North Carolina
Leaving England forever

and heard his children cry
for freedom with his last
dime...he

gave his African queen twelve seeds
of promise planted deep before
slavery ended...and I
promised him honor and freedom

I am a Black man
proud as a Lombardy poplar
stronger than granddaddy's roots
defying place
and time
and history
        crucified

    alive

        immortal

**Look at me and be
healed**

Blackberries, Chocolate Cake and Vanilla Ice Cream in America

I tasted freedom and
picked blackberries with
Huckleberry Finn and drank
water from the Mississippi.
I accompanied Abe Lincoln
to the Ford Theatre.
Across the street I sipped
wine and ate bread.
I dreamed of the 13th
and 14th Amendments
satisfying my hunger
and of a U.S. President quenching
my thirst for freedom.
I am still hungry.

Black People

—whose ancestors suffered during the Middle Passage
To land in America filled with hopelessness,
Who lost the gift of freedom from Africa,
Each working in kitchens and fields,

Giants of strength and nobility
Whose hands and heads taught a country
Emancipation that fought racism,
Gave us will to make it, fight or die—

We bore freedom-fighter children,
Sacrificed our blood against hatred
Of cancerous oppression and stupid wars
Dying with dignity and proud

When with their hypocrisy and devilment,
The enemies seemed determined to destroy
Our minds and hearts that had the capability
To build a people. They battle us now in the 90's.

Poverty. Welfare. Affirmative Action. Prisons.
Crack babies. But we hold on.
We live on.
Defiant until the end of the world.

Race

They grin at blackness
I am brown sugar
High yellow is revered.

Do they know
my brown flesh still burns
like charcoals from their whips
and chains?
Their hungry dogs' saliva
foamed to garble strewn
meat, to taste hot blood,
running like cold water.

They call it history now.
Where are their griefs
to match my pain?
South African whites do not know.
They do not know.

Yet they smile.

For the Love of Freedom

Read your dark history
Bleeding Black people;
Study your enemies' past
All about their white hoods;
Rip these pages from textbooks;
Burn them in enemies' hearts;
Replace them with the love of freedom.

Celebrate

Black History
Every month
Of the year
And stretch your
Mind before
Another Revolution
Comes!

Medgar Evers

Born and educated in Mississippi
He studied law and
Became active in civil rights.
He traveled night and day
Pleading for freedom.
Though he was cut down
In his driveway
His truth kept
Marching on.

Martin Luther King, Jr.

Year after
    year my
        friends remember King
           for his causes—

freedom and justice
    love, hope, and change
        needed now
           Communion and Prayer;

come, King!
    Heaven! Send him,
        his spirit
           to the bowels of the earth

to cleanse,
    coercing racists
        to vomit their evil
           from the past and present

purify souls, renew the earth
    we must remember King,
        police dogs, cold blood,
           black children bombed,

The Mississippi Burning,
    and how bullets
        find apostles and presidents
        and kings;

we must remember
        Montgomery and Memphis,
           the beginning and end,

we must remember
      we must remember
        we must remember
          The Dream.

Emmett Till

You fought yourself out of
your mother's bloody womb,

battled polio at an early age.
You did not know Carolyn Bryant

until she accused you of bad language
you suffered a kidnapping

by Carolyn's husband and buddies
and were baptized in a swamp in Mississippi.

The 75 pound cotton gin
fan sank you in the river.

Your face shown in <u>Jet Magazine</u>
made tears flood American cities.

The world shook in 1955.
Mississippi's soul stained,

You returned to the bowels
of the earth and ate worms.

You flew to Heaven
for perfect peace and understanding.

Americans said you died nobly
impervious to the courtroom farce,

the universe shocked by the exoneration

of the guilty ones who murdered you.
People sang at your funeral,
lined the streets in Chicago,

viewed you one last time
before throngs fainted

some crying uncontrollably with
your mother Mamie in church.

Racism and hatred burned to ashes
that day while you watched from Heaven.

You whistled "God forgive America,
land where I died,"

stand beside her and guide
her from the night

to the light from above.
"God forgive America."

You read your scripture,
"Vengeance is mine, said

the Lord, I will repay."
The devil raked coals

in Hell waiting for more rednecks
and bigots and haters.

You now fly all over God's Heaven
Happy!

The Black Man Speaks of Rivers, Part 2:

A Tribute to Langston Hughes

'I've known rivers':
'I've known rivers' current 'as the world.'

'My soul grows deep like the rivers.'

I listened to Stokely Carmichael
     When furious fire heated cool air.
I shook hands with Martin Luther King, Jr.,
     Before garbage cans in Memphis.
I heard shots in Dallas
     when John F. Kennedy waved at me.

'I've known rivers.'

I heard the drums of stomachs in New York
     when welfare queens paraded the streets.
I danced to the melody of Diana Ross
     when Leontyne Price sang at the Met.
I read Sunday school lessons at home
     when Alice Walker wrote *The Color Purple.*

'I've known rivers.'

I bathed the body of a Rolls Royce
     when shacks cuddled me with love.
I plowed through books at Morehouse College
     when white men perused works at Harvard.
I moved into the mainstream
     a century after Huck and Jim journeyed down the

Mississippi.

'My soul grows deep like the rivers.'

God Put a Rainbow in the Sky

All over the country,
Only glimmers of light appear,
It is cloudy everywhere. Suddenly,
tornadoes destroy homes, the trees
are down, rivers flood the
land with our tears, until the doves
fly away.

Lightning crackles the earth
as rain falls for days.
After the storm ends,
I see a rainbow in the sky
and fall on my knees,
and bow my head
barely able to mumble a word.

Acquaintances

I meet an acquaintance
whose greeting is icy.
Good evening. I am this,
I am that.
And how about you?
I am me.
My desire to explore her heart and soul
through Antarctica is boundless.
The ice melts.
There is no past.
Here we are,
discovering each other's worlds.
Another continent comes between us:
my mahogany skin, her ivory face,
my wooly hair, her lips of wine
create barriers between us as we go.

Noiseless and impatient, we move to darker
regions of the soul.

Words. Now she has them. She wants more.

Black and Beautiful

I am African-American,
Poet of my people,
Black and beautiful,
Sweeter than chocolate candy
Lover of my queen,
Father of my child,
Conscious of my heritage,
Feet tired and hurting,
Attacked because I'm African,
Rejected because I'm Black,
Despised because I'm proud.
But I smile.
I am Black.
I am beautiful.
I am bad.
Just look at me.

The Black Hair

I have just combed woolly hair,
    Nappy and black,
    Refusing to cooperate,
    Resisting stiff grease,
    Kinky,
    Sensitive,
    Curly.
Why, beautiful hair, are you defiant?
And why are you not free?

James Baldwin

He wrote it all
Beginning at age fourteen,
Preaching in the pulpit,
Telling it all on the mountain,
Conflicting with his stepfather.
His books and essays showed
Him strutting his stuff,
Burning with truth,
Sharing family joys and sorrows.
We now know his name.
Oh, if he would only talk now!

Gwendolyn Brooks

Your stately stroll toward me
    kindles a flame of poetic fire.
Your coal blackness and wine blood
    increase your strength
    and inordinate beauty.
Your laughter hides historical pain.

You are life celebrated!

You are the Mother of Blackness
    and Ethnicity and Majesty.
You share your power with the Earth:
We must learn the strength of your love.
Your affection is the base for our being.

You have known suffering and sacrifice
    and oppression and strength.
An African King shares his need for you
    from afar.
Your Blackness must permeate the Universe.

YOU ARE!

The Black Madonna

picking cotton on
a cold day blisters
decorated her black fingers
in the fields

She crawled on her knees
until the sun bowed
to her. Eight children
planted beneath the stars
The earth felt good to her.

You can see her now
a parched face and folded hands
she kneels in a different place
drinking blood and eating bread
at the altar

Comforted
white gloves feel good to her
waving to touch the sky
hymns fill the air
They feel good to her
They feel good to her

On the Death of Mothers

We shall not all meet them robed in Heaven,
Nor see ourselves with crowns of glory;
If anything, in the heat of the night,
Coming with pitchforks and sharp horns,
He will steal unsaved souls.
Come, Light, let us curse the darkness.

Don't Know Why

Sometimes I cry and don't know why,
Sometimes I laugh and almost die.
Then I cry and cry and cry.
Being Black is going to make me die.

The Anniversary

At church
she'd bow to guest preachers
listening
to their hellfire sermons
her wig resting like graveyard grass
the preacher her half sat near her
in tails like a statue
in a cemetery.

And celebrating his anniversary
he'd dream of silver watching it
rovingly, rovingly
as members dropped it in plates
on Jesus' table.

His heart wild with greed
his money, his church, his anniversary
these belonged to others as well.

Special seats establishing his hierarchy
he'd listen for hours
to hoarse voices singing
to praises from peasants
exalting him and her.

Grinning in the light
and quiet
he'd preach next Sunday
the powerful word
the Bible
tight in his fist.

Elegy for Therman B. O'Daniel

I remember his voice, rich and golden;
And his urbane manner, majestic as a king;
And how, once meeting, a smile leaped for us,
And he thundered beliefs about journals and words
And how they last.
We sang, too, his melodies
And dreamed,
Our leafs turning to poems and stories;
Our songs tremble their criticism now.

He kindled an eternal flame
That burns hearts, young and old,
And sacrificed twilight years for stars,
And enjoyed the sunrise and sunsets.

If only we could assure him now
That his work reaped harvests for all seasons,
The fruit of his labors save the world.

Cat

Among animals
and humans
I love the cat black
in a lap
on a cold
day
lying
still
eyes closed
to a crackling fire
and golden flames
free.

A Child's Play

There is a backyard
surrounded
with fences

of different sorts
in a city
on a hill

where a girl
jumps
rope and

inhales air
for a song
circling herself

she hops
on blades
of grass

dying in her
steps; she
ascends her height

the sky
her limit
for joy

His Professor

His hair silk
from rich years
his teachings,
quiet words, I observed:

his slow talk, his
humped shoulders and
head bowed;
his breath short

The books grasped
as if gold
under his arms
resting on yellow notes

published articles,
poems, rhythm;
performing symbols
pupils learn

his labors and
whispers
almost
gone.

And Want No More

To see her in bed
is to know
      the meaning of pain.

It's to understand a surgeon's
scalpel and why.
      How I wish,

desiring her luscious breast, its
nipple now gone with cancerous
      tissue, my kissing it before, teaching

me. Beauty is something deeper
that she is a person
      that love tests

How I loved the breast that
nurtured my child,
      its milk dripped on pillows

I have sinned,
worshipping selfish needs,

a honey-brown breast, now
soaking in blood,
      is like testicles removed.

How humble I am,
one breast left
      giving us more love, the same

To see a wife's breast disfigured,
cancerous cells gone
      is to know wellness

and its shared meaning
is to prolong life
      and want no more.

Rain

The rain kisses
a cold tin roof.

It tinkles making
music and magic
as mother and child
alone hug the night.

A Plea for Peace

Let the hawk roost near
the dove
and their eyes
be mirrors, bright and shining, slow
to shut, quick to trust,
sleepless.
—lifting olive branches to travel
the sky and the land.
Silent (No message
but peace) Fly!

Before the Death of Dad

Before maggots suck your marble eyes,
before bones yield to a hollow earth, inviting
black meat to heat cold blood,

I will tell you of the dark days of youth,
of the tears soaking white pillows, of your
hollers inflicting severe pain. I still

love you, the eldest child from your fruitful
penis, your lost sheep destined to lead; I
touch you in your white casket, when I,

nearly 40, still hunger for your laughter
and ache for honeyed words. Open your eyes
in church, hear the voice of your son:

"Plant me again in my mother's womb."

Embden Pond

As I sat on a pier
Silently kissing a mirror pond,
Waves hushed a banked stillness.
Beyond acres of water
Sailed a two-passenger boat
Through dark tree shadows
Roaring toward the mountain
Leaving behind a world, so new.

Fifty Years of Matrimony

You accepted my brave telephone calls
when I tried to court you for marriage.
We flew kites together and rode bicycles
and you stopped to kiss me to
tell me "I love you."
Your black hair was long
when I used my nervous hands to comb it.
Your eyes met mine like stars
yielding to the bloody moon.
We would have good times
and bad times living and loving
producing a precious Princess
who would cement the three of us.
She had her cross to bear
at an early age but
God kept her close to Him
while He healed you of
your breast cancer and brain tumor.
You kept driving your red car
to your good church where
your pastor prayed for your
continued healing.
I suffered later not
knowing whether I would live
or die. God intervened
and healed me, too,
to be with you a bit
longer. He was our miracle doctor.
Princess stood by us
both as she directed children's
music at her school reminding

us all that love
conquers pain
and sorrow and suffering.
We sat together yearly at South Beach
at Martha's Vineyard,
where twenty-five years
of visits replenished
our spirits and sustained
us and healed us.
Our love for fifty years conquered all.

Flowers and Flies

In this green yard of summer
There grew hundreds of flowers
Waiting for pollination
And bees hunting for nectar
Yucca Moths pollinate Yucca flowers
Laying their eggs on the base of fig flowers,
Houseflies search for food with
Their eyes acting as prisms
Breaking light into an array of colors.
Earth has flowers and flies
Everywhere in summer
Gladiolus and roses,
Morning Glories and Snapdragons,
Oriental Poppies and Transvaal Daisies,
Houseflies and Horseflies and Bumblebees
And I, a country boy
Looking out my front window,
Admiring the beauty of flowers
And the army of flies that
Make love to them,
Wish that I might fly toward the moon
And worship forever the joy of Heaven
Where flowers and flies welcome me.

Why I Will Not be a Child Again

My demons hide
like ghosts after dark:
there is no fear
of light. I will curse
like them the rest
of my life, even
beyond the grave.
Childhood memories make
a hell for adult goodness.
I am lonely in church.
I am eccentric at home.

It is winter.
I feel cold.
I see my child
sleigh riding,
cutting acres of snow.
I am the river.
I am the mountain.
I am the forest.

My soul catches fire—
I am the sun.
I am the moon.
I am a morning star.

I Fly Away

Sometimes
after church service,
I talk to white folk
My black suit is so dapper.
My wide straw hat
fights the hot sun
while I sip lemonade
and laugh
with blacks and whites
savoring social intercourse
under a Maple tree.
I am cool, cool, so cool.
Then Miss Manners points
to my "fly" in public,
asking,
"What's that you've got there?"
Half my shirt rests outside my pants.
I quickly pull my shirt
inside the proper place.
Laughter from the crowd
accompanies my embarrassment.
Miss Manners is secure now,
having bruised an ego,
evoked laughter, and
tasted power.
She turns red with her smile
and walks away
with her other half.
I strut in the opposite direction,
black and beautiful and proud
of what she did not know.

Neglecting the Flowers

I work until
midnight, checking
students' papers,
kissing the moon
until cocks crow.

I write in corners
where silence
speaks loudly
and words drip
honey,

sweetening the
days filled with
sorrow. They say
I labor too hard,
teaching and writing,

neglecting the
flowers
struggling
for growth
at home.

The Whipping Song

The Cardinal at my window
sings blood in my veins.
I will tell anyone who asks,
it's made my heart leap, for
who can resist songs at morning?
His clothes burn the Celestial
sun. His quickness arouses
dull senses. If I stare in
his eyes, I am his slave, yielding
to his beauty, whipped by his song.

Birds

Seven days, each night
Red, blue, and black birds
Land on our front porch,
Hunting seeds by their feeder,
    As if at home.

Awed a million times, the birds
Whistle first; then the melody of their voices!
Singing at dawn and eventide,
They pause and spy for security,
    As if freedom were elusive.

Their presence is observed daily,
When neighbors open curtains,
To praise their congregation,
To savor a serenade in the air,
    As if yearning for communion.

Is it rare to have birds,
Acquaintances, suspicious of motives,
Seek trust and safety here—
to eat, sing, and touch humanity,
    As if time were to die?

Be Like the Flower

Be like the flower, which
Blossoming on dark days
Stands erect with pride
Withstands the heavy rain
Yet opens
Knowing it has beauty.

Working on the Farm in 1947

On the farm he learned
at five-years-old the mule's
obedience to pull while
he too short steps to
hold the plow steady
and follow.
It was the post-war years
for the world but his father
had land which needed
breaking.

Black people were farming
everywhere in the South
where cotton was king.
Even in the woods, their land,
they dynamited stumps clearing
the way for planting.
In winter weather he skipped school
to pick cotton from sharp bolls –
trembled with cold, a sign of
weakness he was told.

December 24th was Santa Claus time
in their white house on a hill,
nine children in bed warmed their
bodies, hearts beating with fear.
When morning came one bicycle and
one doll baby hugged the Christmas
tree waiting to surprise everyone.

He the eldest rode the bicycle first

down the hill from home was told,
"Don't ride too far. It's dangerous!"
So he rode slowly down the path
and lost control riding himself into
the cotton patch
Falling.

Up again he rode back home the hill
hard to climb.
Falling again. Cotton fields watched
and waited.

The sun went down.
Morning. Cotton acres greeted him.
Another day of cotton picking.
Another day to dream of school.
The doll baby cried.

Fire and Fury

"The water from one bucket, thrown by one man,
couldn't douse the flames that shot from the
neighborhood store."

"Fire and Fury"
<u>Newsweek</u>, 11 May 1992

Black men with the sound of cracked bones
Are falling down. I see one spitting America
Fire and fury to protest a police stick,
And he gets up and down, calling, "O God."
My country eyes videos in black and white,
And stupid animals, brutal, suck blood,
While a man eats dirt and burns cities,
Then reads James Baldwin's <u>The Fire Next Time</u>.

Jazz After Dinner

On a snowy evening I shall feel his sounds,
Quietly moaning, inviting cold air to listen,
Call pleasure from golden keys. Old friends
Will kiss their company, sit to relax and dream.
And music, crying, like an elderly man
That sometime after sunrise greets the morning
Will pervade the world, profusely fill
That evening and me, celebrating life.

The Sad Adult

Past, stay behind him,
the night once cried,
the fighting physical
between husband and wife.

Has the heart healed
from the childhood years
and the dark secret
buried now risen from the grave?

Poem from the Farm

Eleven of us picked cotton in the fields,
children, mother, and father on those
days when winter brought snow
across the already white fields
and chilled our eyes and ears
so cold were we that bad
weather blessed us with ice storms.
Christmas Eve came.
We dreamed and warmed ourselves
by the fireplace, ate candy canes
and waited for Santa Claus.

Where Grandma Used to Live

Grandma's house sat back
From the road near juke joints
Where blues songs could be heard
And drunkards cursed the dilapidated building.
Neighbors thought it sinful
To dance and sing the blues.
Money earned paid for Miss Miner's
Daughter's college tuition.
Townspeople found it
Difficult to send anyone to college
During the Depression.
Well, Miss Miner's daughter
Graduated with honors.
Miss Miner arrived at church
Early Sunday morning to
Thank God for juke joints
Where Grandma used to live.

What Black Parents Named Us

From slavery until the present,
Our names have been secular
and sacred:
From David to Jezebel,
Moody Askew to Aunt Lizzie Pearl,
Miss Addy to Mr. Leander,
Aunt Melissie to Uncle Zechariah,
Peachick to Zebedee,
Miss Doshie to Uncle Thaddeus,
Walter Nathaniel to Henrietta Bonaparte,
Uncle "Nut" to Uncle "Pecan,"
Aunt Queenie to Aunt Snuke,
"C" to June "Bug,"
"Boo" to Vergie Mae,
Aunt Malinda to Aunt Martha,
Grandpa Cola to Grandma Meather,
Grandpa Will to Grandma Claudia,
Jamal to Sesquita Zaleika.
What's in a name?
A history and culture
Rich in love
Indomitable in spirit.

Molly

She struts the fields sunrise to sunset
Pulling the plow that cuts black soil. I
Hold the handles as sweat falls,
And pull her ropes right and left.
She huffs and puffs and pulls.
Five years old, I run and follow
Now stop to rub her nose and ears,
Her breath bad and hot with foam.
I lead her to water where
She thinks and drinks
To fill her belly to relieve the pain.
Molly my friend my pet my all
Proudly plows deep and long
Then leans to Mother Earth
To taste delicious worms.

Music on My Radio at 5 A.M.

Softly, by the fireplace, Bach is performing for me;
Taking me back to college days, when I was required
To listen to classical music on Saturday afternoons
And fulfill Music 101 requirements, taking notes on Mozart

And Beethoven at 5 A.M., the violin crying for love
And attention wakes Verdi from the grave, his heart now beats
To the old Saturday afternoon music in college, with snow outside
And notes in the air, the radio announcer my guide.

So now I wait for Handel to lift my soul
With the great arias of the past. The music
Of college days wakes me, my body is responding
In the depth of remembrance, I pray on my knees
to be worthy today of this beauty and joy.

My poems! All painful memories, tears, and sorrow!

My poems! All painful memories, tears, and sorrow!
And somehow they keep me writing
About the possible beauty somewhere in the world
Maybe in the woods where deer roam.
This walk – I wish I could find flowers
In winter, or any season
To rescue me from self pity
Yet I know better than
To weep as if I did not have God
In my life to guide me daily.
I am His child – and I
Depend on Him for strength
To keep taking my journeys
In life where He leads me.
O Darling my words have you
I dare not complain anymore.

Memories for Posterity

The white school building had closed
In the 1950's because of low enrollment.
Three teachers who taught seven grades
Now transferred to a bigger school
Where black students learned
And were whipped less often.
The first grade teacher had pinched
Students' ears in the closed white school building,
The second grade teacher had whipped
Students until their legs were swollen
With blood running profusely down
Their legs landing in their shoes.
The seventh grade teacher had
Beaten a student on the back until
His back became bigger with welts
That looked like a slave's beaten back.
The teacher laughed at him
When students complained
That he was in excruciating pain.

Well, these three teachers are dead now
And former students contributed money
To renovate the building as a community center.
The colorful paint and refurbished rooms
Would not erase the memory of these three cruel teachers
Who inflicted pain on innocent children
Who were chastised for not learning.
Years later choirs would sing God's praises.
Continuing adult education courses and
Voting for political candidates
Would not destroy the ghosts

That visited the old white school
Where the community depended on outsiders
To keep memories alive with a museum,
Their not realizing that the building
Would be demolished thirty years later
Because of the death of former students
Who had passed the torch to the community
A painful past buried in the graves.
Green grass grew on the old land,
Flowers bloomed everywhere,
The community celebrated.

What It's Like to be a Black Professor

First, it's Heaven and Hell and
absorbing pain daily, like being
tortured for the good you're doing,
like celebrating when right triumphs,
it's loving everyone and trusting no one,
meeting beautiful colleagues, friendly
and ugly bastards who forget those
who have helped them professionally,
and dealing with persons who gain
weight sitting, not lifting a finger
to earn their salaries, but wasting
time socializing with visitors, it's
finding beauty and truth, good and
bad in and outside classrooms, and
forgiving your enemies but not for-
getting their names, it's sharing goals
and objectives, wearing clean clothes
and smelling good, and starting on
time and ending on time, not watching
the clock before departure time, it's
fire and fervor and the academy re-
warding faculty and students for
excellence, it's finally being grateful
for the gift to lead and serve in the
best place in the world
before saying goodbye.

The Red Bicycle

I want to ride
      my red bicycle
so I can exercise
      for longevity.
What good am I
      dead
when I can delay
      peddling
my way
      to Heaven?

The Red Dog

The red dog
ran to the
black mailbox
biting the mail carrier's
leg until he
dropped all mail
and ran away
the dog satisfied

Anger in the South

Mean,
That a white-looking Negro,
Principal of an elementary school
In the good old South
In the 1960's
Would tell his former student,
Now a college professor
That his boss
Was nothing but an old nigger!

The Wind

Its mighty power can destroy homes
And break hearts and bring tears
To the rich and poor
Can blow cars in the sky,

Split trees into splinters,
Lift bodies from the ground
Turn them around and around.
Airplanes can fall from Heaven
Joggers can run to ravines.
Its great strength can humble the earth

Make victims start again from scratch
Build unity from adversity
Remind the world of the
Fear and power of God.

Rules and Rituals

They marched to the altar
Erect and solemn
Dressed in their garb for the Lord.
Because they were ordained,
They showed commoners in the audience
What beautiful cloth looked like.
They strut their stuff for the Lord.
They worshipped and read
And bowed and kneeled.
Academic attire was frowned upon
Unless it was for Lessons and Carols
And not for Christmas Eve.
Commoners participating
Wore plain clothes to the altar
And to the lectern to read.
Some forgot that commoners were also
Ordained by God to be Lectors
And Disciples free to wear
What God wanted.
God judges all hearts,
Not outward appearances.
He said, "Come to me just as you are."
The Devil said, "I love
Stratification and racism,
Sexism and ageism,
Xenophobia and homophobia.
Close your church doors forever.
Be pretty and follow me."

Readers in Church

Readers in church
Walk to the Eagle
The <u>Bible</u> rests precariously
On the podium.

Half of the stand had a hole
Lectors fear moving it
Right or left so that
They could read in a modicum of light.

The lamp had died
For some time now
And the electrical outlet
Took the blame.

And the minister on his side
Had a bright lamp
Perfect to see the Word
For him to preach.

Not until the <u>Bible</u> fell
Through the hole on the reader's side
And he caught it
Proceeding to read with grace

Then the congregation noticed
That darkness could become light
When God communicates
Fix what is wrong with His church.

Reverend Hot Air

You preached that people
 Should treat others the way
They want to be treated.
You hooped and hollered
Until balls of sweat
Popped from your forehead.

You ran up and down the aisle
 Raising your hand to Heaven
And fell on your knees
Preaching the Word. Ahaa!

Then one night in a motel
Deacon Goodwin's wife
Gave you a horseback ride
And you rode too fast.

To preach the Word
Is to live the Word
Before dying.

Pure Light

In the evening were the glowing
moon and shining stars, a gift
moving the world. Brighter
now, rays of light,
glimmer of hope; unborn child
on a donkey sleeping in darkness.
We were falling in
Eden, Virgin Mother.
We were waiting on edge
for a new world, for centuries:
praying for you to give birth to
new love and pure light.

The Preacher

Where sinners gather, the poem
weeps. The poem begs
that the truth will not hurt.
He bragged about his automobiles
Cadillac Jaguar Mercedes Benz
about his house as big as the White House
about his wealthy professional members
of his congregation who gave
him a $10,000.00 Anniversary Gift
about his desire to purchase a
50 million dollar airplane
to spread the Gospel.
He forgot about the homeless
starving people all over the world
about the poor in spirit.
He forgot about Matthew
Mark Luke John and Paul.
He preached and preached
with great balls of fire
that all should take up their
cross and follow him.

Questions Asked Me Over the Years

Questions asked me
By a preacher:
"Just how did you get to go to college?"

By a former professor:
"Just how did you get an invitation to read at Harvard?"

By a Fisk University alumna:
"Just how did you get to know Ralph Ellison?"

By a former white colleague who could not earn his Ph.D. degree in English:
"Just how were you able to get your Ph.D. degree in English?"

By a so called friend:
"Just how did you get hired as a full professor with tenure at The State University of New York at Albany?"

By a dear relative:
"Just how were you able to publish so many books?"

By a favorite cousin:
"Just how were you able to attend your mother's funeral at a time conflicting with your wife's major surgery and succeed in doing both?"

By a fraternity brother:
"Just how have you been able to forgive your enemies, love God, and obey His Commandments before knocking the hell out of somebody?"

Why He Went to College

If he hadn't,
his oldest brother
would have worn suits
after college graduation
he said;
he refused to have
him surpass him.
He graduated without
college going through
him saying he
learned nothing,
yet he enjoyed his
big salary working
for travel to the
moon people.
His rewards?
his Mercedes Benz,
his house bigger
than the White House
ribeye steak for dinner,
his trips all over the world.
He forgot his humble
origins on the farm
where he could have remained,
walking in mule and
cow dung,
feeding the pigs,
milking cows,
plowing in the fields
from sunrise to sunset;
for whatever reasons

he became anti-intellectual
envying educators
and co-workers who
surpassed him earning
their graduate and professional
degrees.
He wanted to be the
family patriarch.
Death wanted him in
the hospital but gave
him another chance
to be reborn or
to burn in Hell.

What Some College Students Told Me

That I was too hard as a professor.
That they did not know why
      they should know grammar.
That they do not read newspapers.
That it is better to cheat
      than to repeat.
That I should have been a preacher.
That I loved to hear myself talk.
That I graded too hard.
That some students were afraid of me.
That I was one of the meanest
      professors they've ever had.
That some students were stabbing
      me in the back.
That some faculty members
      were jealous of me.
That some administrators see
      me as a threat.
That they wish they had a
      husband like me.
That I should have been
      a college president.
That I was no John Keats
      as a writer.
That I use the power of
      the pen to get my enemies.
That I know how to forgive
      but I do not forget.
That I am more loyal
      to people than they are to me.
That I work too hard.

That I am generous to a fault.
That I want more
      for my students than
      they want for themselves.
That I love teaching.

Beautiful Black Women

I can't help talking about something
about their beautiful skin
black women
with their brilliant minds
leading colleges and universities
achieving and believing and changing
the quality of our communities and world
teaching students with fire
administering and serving and supporting
walking with purposefulness
driving their old cars and new cars
wearing their professional clothes
and exquisite jewelry
putting on appropriate perfume
strutting their stuff in high heels and low heels
and I smile and sing
admiring their black hair
watch their lips speak truth
study their eyes, mirrors to their souls
their gift of scrumptious food
that communicates love
where family and friends gather
and I rejoice and pray
for more beautiful gifted powerful
black women
with their resilience,
their whole being immortalized

Opray Winfrey

She shares her wealth with the world;
Her childhood never forgotten,
One opportunity after another presents itself
While she works assiduously—always giving.

She helps Africans and others educate themselves,
Not for fame or glory defying description.
But for larger causes creating sweetness and light,
She teaches like professors in colleges and universities,
Inspires and motivates and guides for the love and joy
Of it all. She reads Scripture daily and prays for all.
She remains the beautiful Queen of Giving and sharing
With <u>The Butler</u> and <u>Greenleaf</u> and <u>The Color Purple</u>
She makes an indelible mark on a culture black and beautiful,
Movies and magazines rooted in the sacred and the secular,
Flowers from the global community shower and elevate
her stature.
Angels in Heaven sing her praises and her greatness,
Our Queen of the Universe anointed to help save our world.

Barack Obama

After such campaigns – what results?
What demarcation of votes? (to find
Among some regions rebelliousness that
Frightens freedom achieved based on merit.)

The Vision of America.
Model of rainbow coalitions:
Model of our desired equality:
Even the bloody history of our suffering.

We see rights ancestors died for.
We seek Paradise here: flowers, sunlight,
Clouds, the rain for growth and harvest
In this new century of all colors.

We seek morning stars.
A triumph of noble spirit.
We see our gifts and our leader.
Redeemed America. And Obama.

There Will Be Blacks in Heaven

There will be blacks to teach
what others don't know.

There will be Cleopatra who will
smile as she removes her crown for sleep
on a moving cloud.

There will be Haile Selassie whose
beard will be combed by angels
adoring him.

There will be William Wells Brown who will be
revising his novel, *Clotel*, for the making
of a movie among the stars.

There will be Harriet Tubman chatting
with Abe Lincoln about the condition
of blacks back home in 1993, defining
their oppression, injustice, and mental slavery.

There will be Booker T. Washington debating
W.E.B. Du Bois on the progress of blacks
and the value of integration and segregation
in the South during the good old days.

There will be Mary McLeod Bethune advising
Franklin Delano Roosevelt to speak to Bill Clinton
about the value of historically black colleges.

There will be Martin Luther King, Jr., in front
of Malcolm X, shouting to throngs,

"Free at last!
Free at last!
Thank God Almighty,
Free at last!"

Lessons Remembered

I learned how to pray
from my religious father.
He prayed passionately from
his heart at annual revivals
until he died at 93.
"The communication is between
you and God," he taught me.

He sang in the choir behind
the pulpit until he volunteered
prayer at one annual revival.
During the revival the preacher rose
to tell him after his prayer that he did not know
how to pray and critiqued him.
"I was not talking to you;
I was talking to the Lord,"
he said loudly and repeatedly
until the preacher's criticism ceased.
The preacher left church with
his butt whipped and his sermon forgotten.

The Country Preacher's Folk Prayer

Eternal God,
We come this mornin'
with bowed heads and humble hearts.

    Uh hum.

We thank you for sparing us another day
by letting your angels watch over our
bedside while we slumbered and slept.

    Uh hum.

We come to you without any form or fashion:
just as we are without one plea.

    Uh hum.

You blessed us when we didn't deserve it.
When we traveled down the road of sin,
you snatched us, and made us tasted of the
blood of Thy Lamb.

    Yes, Lord!

This mornin', touch every human heart.
Transform tears into Heavenly showers
for the salvation of sinful souls.

    Yassir.

Remember the sick, the afflicted,

the heavy laden.
Open the windows of Thy Heavenly home.
Let perpetual light shine on them in the midnight hour.

Yes, Lord.

When we have done all that we can do down here,
take us into Thy kingdom, where the sun never sets,
where there's no more bigotry, hypocrisy, backbiting;
no more weeping and wailing, before Thy throne, where
you will wipe away our tears; where we can see our
mothers;

I want my Mama!

Where, in that city, where the streets are paved in gold and
adorned with every jewel,
where we can see Jesus, sitting on the throne
of glory.

Ummmm mmmmmm a hummmmmmm.

When we get home, when we get home,
when we get home,

we'll rest in Thy bosom
and praise you forever.

Amen

Acknowledgments

Many thanks to the editors of the following works, in which some poems were previously published. They are published by permission of the author.

The Griot: Journal of the Southern Conference on African American Studies
Catalyst
The Zora Neale Hurston Forum
The Kentucky Poetry Review
The Black Scholar
Prophetic Voices: International Literary Journal
Testimony
The Courier-Journal
The Little Magazine
Essence Magazine
KOLA Magazine (Canada)
Classique
I, Too, Am America
I Fly Like a Bird
The Whipping Song
Vintage
Pure Light
Neglecting the Flower
Lilacs in Spring
For the Love of Freedom
Jazz After Dinner
Poems for People of All Ages
God Put a Rainbow in the Sky

Sweet Solitude
The Boulé Journal

Gratitude and Inspiration

Many thanks to my mentor, Dr. George Hendrick, former Chair of the Department of English at the University of Illinois at Urbana-Champaign and currently University Research Professor at Stony Brook University (SUNY), without whom this manuscript would not have been born; Roberta Hall Slade, my good wife and best friend of 52 years, whose encouragement sustains me; Minitria Elisabeth Slade, my daughter, whose support of my arts and letters gives me faith and hope for a better world; Dr. Oscar Williams, former Chair of the Department of Africana Studies at the University at Albany (SUNY), whose respect for my work inspires me to keep writing and publishing for present and future generations; Raymond M. Burse, brilliant attorney, who motivates me to work hard for rewarding results; Paul Grondahl, prolific author, who sets high standards for all writers; Marcy Casavant, whose impeccable technical work on this manuscript gave it richness and palatableness; Rex Smith, Editor and Vice President of the Times Union, who demonstrates the power of the word with beauty and truth; Amy Bianccoli, inimitable author, whose mastery of the writing craft objectifies ideas with aims toward perfection; and President Havidan Rodriguez, of the University at Albany (SUNY), whose support of my creative writing keeps me rooted intellectually and professionally for the light of the world.

Leonard A. Slade, Jr.

L eonard A. Slade, Jr. received the bachelor's degree in English from North Carolina's Elizabeth City State University of the University of North Carolina System, the master's degree in English from Virginia State University, and the Ph.D. degree in English from the University of Illinois at Urbana-Champaign. He taught for twenty-two years at Kentucky State University, where he was Chair of the Department of Literature, Languages, and Philosophy, Director of the Division of Humanities and Fine Arts, and Dean of the College of Arts and Sciences. In May 1989, Kentucky State University awarded him the degree Doctor of Humane Letters. In May 1996, Elizabeth City State University of the University of North Carolina System awarded him a Doctor of Humane Letters degree. He studied at the University of Ghana in West Africa. For Several summers, he studied poetry at Bennington College, Vermont; at the Bread Loaf Writers' Conference, Middlebury College, Vermont; at the Ragdale Artists' Colony, Lake Forest, Illinois; and as a Poet Fellow at the Martha's Vineyard Institute of Creative Writing in Poetry and Fiction. He studied with Pulitzer Prize winners Stephen Dunn and Donald Justice. Slade also studied African-American Literature with Richard Bardsdale (M.A., Ph.D. in English, Harvard University) at the University of Illinois at Urbana-Champaign; Keneth Kinnamon (M.A., Ph.D. in English, Harvard University) at the University of Illinois at Urbana-Champaign; and Edward Davidson (Ph.D. in English, Yale University and a Guggenheim Fellow) at the University of Illinois at Urbana-Champaign. Slade's Dissertation Advisor was George Hendrick (Ph.D. in English, University of Texas, Austin) at the University of Illinois at Urbana-Champaign, where Hendrick was Chair of the Department of English and a Pulitzer Prize nominee.

He has published in *Essence Magazine, U.S. News and World Report, The Courier-Journal, Ebony Magazine, The College Language Association Journal, The American Poetry Review, The Zora Neale Hurston Forum, The English Journal: Publication of the National Council of Teachers of English, The Journal of Southern History, The Black Scholar, The Kentucky Poetry Review, KOLA Magazine* (in Canada), *Emerge Magazine, The Journal of Blacks in Higher Education, Catalyst, The ALAN Review: Publication of the National Council of Teachers of English, Little Magazine, The Griot: Journal of the Southern Conference on African-American Studies, Peace and Freedom Journal* (The United Kingdom), and *Education Next: Journal of Opinion and Research at Harvard University*, to name a few. He has published twenty-six books, including twenty-one books of poetry: *Another Black Voice: A Different Drummer* (1988), *The Beauty of Blackness* (1989), *I Fly Like a Bird* (1992), *The Whipping Song* (1993), *Vintage* (1995), *Fire Burning* (1995), *Pure Light* (1996), *Neglecting the Flowers* (1997), *Lilacs in Spring* (1998), *Elisabeth and Other Poems* (1999), *For the Love of Freedom* (2000), *Jazz After Dinner* (2006), *Triumph* (2010), *Sweet Solitude* (State University of New York Press, 2010), *The Season* (2011), *Chasing the Wind* (2012), *God Put a Rainbow in the Sky* (2014), *Nobody Knows* (2016), *Poems for People of All Ages* (2017), and *I, Too, Am America* (2018). *Sweet Solitude* was a bestseller at the State University of New York Press. *I, Too, Am America* is his twenty-first book of poetry. Slade received the Editor's Choice Award for six of his poems which were published in the *Today's Best Poets Anthology* (Summer

2013). *Symbolism in Herman Melville's Moby Dick: From the Satanic to the Divine* (1998) is his second book of literary criticism. Slade's books have been sold in China, Japan, India, Finland, The Netherlands, The United Kingdom, Germany, France, Denmark, and Italy. He has read his poetry at West Point, Ohio State, Williams College, Skidmore College, Norfolk State, Virginia State, the Universities of Missouri, Kentucky, Tennessee, Virginia, Arkansas, Illinois, Tufts, Duke, and Harvard, among others.

Slade is Professor Emeritus of Africana Studies and English and Past Director of the Humanistic Studies Doctoral Program and of the Master of Arts in Liberal Studies Program at the State University of New York at Albany. He is also the Edmund J. James Scholar in English at the University of Illinois at Urbana-Champaign. He was an Eminent Scholar at Virginia State University. Slade has also taught at Skidmore College, Union College, and RPI in New York. He is former National President of Alpha Kappa Mu Honor Society, as well as former National President of The Langston Hughes Society. In November 2007, he was named Citizen Academic Laureate at SUNY Albany. In April 2005, he was named a Collins Fellow at SUNY Albany. In October 2016, Slade received the Literary Legend Award from the Albany, New York, Public Library. A past member of the National Research Center on the Teaching of Literature, he has been the recipient of the President's Excellence in Teaching Award at Kentucky State University and at the State University of New York, Albany; The Professor of the Year Award from the SUNY NAACP Chapter; The Langston Hughes Society Distinguished Service Award; The Distinguished Service Award from Alpha Kappa Mu National Honor Society; The Kentucky Humanities Council Grant; The Hudson Mohawk Association of Colleges and Universities Award; The Northeast

Modern Language Association Research Fellowship for Poetry; The Martha's Vineyard Institute of Creative Writing in Poetry Fellowship; The Ford Foundation Fellowship; The National Association for Equal Opportunity in Higher Education Award in Washington, D.C.; The U.S. Department of State Fellowship for Postdoctoral Study in West Africa; The Ragdale Artists' Poetry Fellowship; Lake Forest, Illinois; The Southern Conference on African-American Studies Poetry Book Award; The Henry M. Minton Fellow Award from the Boulé; The Kappa Alpha Psi Fraternity's Distinguished Educational Leadership Award; The Poetry Gold Medal of Excellence Award; The Editor's Choice Award from Poetryfest in Oregon; and The Poet of the Year Award from The Institute for Advanced Poetic Studies. Slade is a member of Sigma Tau Delta International English Honor Society, The Modern Language Association, The Southern Conference on African-American Studies, and the College Language Association. Under his leadership as Chair of the Department of Africana Studies, the Master's Program in Africana Studies was ranked number two in America three years in a row (2005, 2006, 2007). He lives with his wife in Albany, New York, and has one daughter.

Praise for Slade's Poetry

"Dr. Leonard A. Slade, Jr., is a gifted poet. His poems that deal with social issues reflect the complexity of people and relationships, as well as highlight some very troubling contemporary problems. Slade's poetry is truly a healing work of art."

Sandra M. Grayson
Professor of English
University of Wisconsin at Milwaukee

"The beauty of Slade's poetry is the adequacy of their feeling and the fine images he discovers for their expressions. His poetry is a rich addition to our literary stores."

Houston A. Baker, Jr.
Distinguished Professor of English
Vanderbilt University

"In spare, unpretentious verse Slade asks us to think about racism, history, love, the beauty of nature, the homeless, old teachers, young daughters, political hypocrisy-- and more. These are splendid, moving poems."

Elizabeth Ammons
Former Dean
The College of Arts and Sciences
Tufts University

"Dr. Leonard A. Slade, Jr.'s poetry presents a historical panorama of American blacks. His poems cover a range of subjects. They reflect the poet's values: family, education, love, nature, the history of blacks in the U.S., hypocrisy, and politics. Slade is a new breed of black poet."

R. Baird Shuman
Professor Emeritus of English
University of Illinois at Urbana-Champaign

CPSIA information can be obtained
at www.ICGtesting.com
Printed in the USA
LVHW012329210221
679514LV00007B/859

9 781662 802690